WITHDRAWN

60489

CONTEMPORARY WRITERS IN CHRISTIAN PERSPECTIVE
EDITED BY RODERICK JELLEMA

Stephen Spender
Louis MacNeice
Cecil Day Lewis

A CRITICAL ESSAY
BY DEREK STANFORD

LIBRARY
BRYAN COLLEGE
DAYTON, TENN. 37321

WILLIAM B. EERDMANS/PUBLISHER

Copyright © 1969 by William B. Eerdmans Publishing Co.
All rights reserved
Library of Congress Catalog Card Number: 67-19315
Printed in the United States of America

I INTRODUCTION

"A particular label"

> The secret of these hills was stone, and cottages
> Of that stone made,
> And crumbling roads
> That turned on sudden hidden villages.
>
> Now over these small hills, they have built the concrete
> That trails black wire;
> Pylons, those pillars
> Bare like nude giant girls that have no secret.

So wrote Stephen Spender in 1933, his poem "The Pylons" providing — as he remarked twenty-one-years later — "a particular label for some of the poetry of the 'Thirties: an embarrassment to my friends' luggage more even than to my own." At the time these verses were written, however, there may have been naivete, as of a child with a new train set, but embarrassment was out of the question. Rimbaud, in the last century, had said that it was "necessary to be absolutely modern"; and Auden, Spender, Day Lewis and MacNeice were all busily bent on taking poetry and making it new. The contemporary look required by the Muse seemed to these young poets partly a matter of reflecting in their poetry the industrial society of their day. Images from the world of machines were particularly favored by them. Thus Spender writes of the noise of the express,

> The song of her whistle screaming at curves,
> Of deafening tunnels, brakes, innumerable bolts,

and, though he has to employ romantic imagery to make his point, insists upon the triumph of the mechanical over the pastoral:

> Ah, like a comet through the flame, she moves entranced,
> Wrapped in her music no bird song, no, nor bough
> Breaking with honey buds shall ever equal.

In a more subtle fashion, Day Lewis uses railway images to express the end of a love-relationship:

> Suppose that we, tomorrow or the next day,
> Came to an end — in storm the shafting broken,
> Or a mistaken signal, the flange lifting —
> Would that be premature, a test for sorrow?

while MacNeice selects urban images to express disintegration and threat in the years between the wars:

> The street is up again, gas, electricity or drains,
> Ever-changing conveniences, nothing comfortable remains
> Un-improved, as flagging Rome improved villa and sewer
> (A sound-proof library and a stable temperature).
>
> Our street is up, red lights sullenly mark
> The long trench of pipes, iron guts in the dark,
> And not till the Goths again come swarming down the hill
> Will cease the clangour of the pneumatic drill.

Such mechanical ornaments as trains, drains, and pylons — though they provided a group name for these poets — were, however, only a small part of their program. The Italian futurists and the Russian Mayakovsky had earlier made much of these devices, while Eliot's first volumes of verse resort to a background use of such means, as adroit and atmospheric as they are unobtrusive: "The memory throws up high and dry/ A crowd of twisted things/... A broken spring in a factory yard," "While I was fishing in the dull canal/ On a winter evening round behind the gashouse."

Turning back to Spender's poem "The Pylons," we see what lay behind this employment of engineering adornments:

> The valley with its gilt and evening look
> And the green chestnut of customary root,
> Are mocked dry like the parched bed of a brook.
>
> But far above and far as sight endures
> Like whips of anger
> With lightning's danger
> There runs the quick perspective of the future.

The sinister potency attributed to the pylons is indicative of the way in which these poets looked at modern existence. The poem brings into sharp collision two ways of life — the past and the future — and suggests how the settled tenor of the first is disturbed and disrupted by the second. The Pylon poets saw how industrial living constituted a challenge to the traditional image of man established within an agrarian ethos. Nor was that challenge a pretty one. A contemporary critic has indicted the period in which these poets wrote as one of "mass unemployment through the world, workers' poverty and homes, humbug from famous people, the importance of money in worldly estimates of worth, the lack of meaning in accepted creeds."

This was certainly how these poets interpreted industrial living in our Western democracies. For Auden, capitalist economy in the slump is represented by those "silted harbours, derelict works" which figure so often in his lines; images to be set against Spender's starry-eyed song of Stakhanovite heroics in what then seemed to the Left a land of promise:

> Death is another milestone on their way.
> With laughter on their lips and with winds blowing round them
>
> They record simply
> How this one excelled all others in making driving belts.

To this perhaps fanciful saga of labor ("This is festivity, it is the time of statistics") Spender opposed his elegy for the unemployed:

> In railway halls, on pavements near the traffic,
> They beg, their eyes made big by empty staring
> And only measuring time, like the blank clock.

Nor was the debate between capitalism and communism the only theme of these poets. Outside, in Germany, there was fascism. As Spender noted:

> Meagre men shoot up. Rockets, rockets,
> A corporal's flaming tongue wags above flaming parliament
>
> The tide of killers now, behold the whip-masters!
> Breeches and gaiters camouflage mud.

while for Auden the war in Spain became an image of the human conscience ("I am your choice, your decision: yes, I am Spain").

Employed superficially, the industrial-mechanical imagery of these poets appeared often as a mere fad or fashion; but when it was used with a deeper sense of the social context it gained significance. Thus, for Auden, the city becomes the locality that best expresses the discrepancy between our way of living and man's fundamental nature:

> In unlighted streets you hide away the appalling
> Factories where lives are made for a temporary use
> Like collars or chairs, rooms where the lonely are battered
> Slowly like pebbles into fortuitous shapes.

Looking at a bust of Apollo, Rilke tells us in his *Sonnets to Orpheus* that the stone head with its accumulated beauty seemed to say to him, "You must change your life." Regarding the Medusan landscape of industrial England in the thirties, with its depressed areas, unemployment and malnutrition, the Pylon poets heard the same admonition. They, too, must change their way of living, and learn to show others, also, how to change.

It is at this point that these poets become of more than historical interest, though our concern with them is related to the history of their times. It has been customary to think of them as revolutionary poets — poets dedicated to a cult of violent political change. It is true that such an hypothesis of action did exist as one element in their work; but anything like a planned program of change appears never to have gained their assent and must certainly be looked for in vain in their verse.

What they *did* insist upon was an internal change — a revolution within the self. "Harrow the house of the dead," wrote Auden, "look shining at / New styles of architecture, a change of heart." Spender realized even more clearly that the individual person is the pivot of change. If revolution is to be transformation, then revolution begins at home. Spiritual implications are obvious here.

> Different living is not living in different places
> But creating in the mind a map
> And willing on the map a desert.
> Pinnacled mountain, or saving resort.

At the same time, the change that these poets stipulated was not envisaged in quietist terms. Their desire was not to create little lonely cells of harmonious living withdrawn from society as a whole and content not to influence its decisions. Instead, they imagined their salvationist words carried like a revivalist's gospel. Essentially they were unconcerned with the isolated perfectionist, paring his spirit's finger nails. Beginning with the "I," they nonetheless contended that "the proper study of mankind is man"; and Michael Roberts, a contemporary critic, noted how their attitude was nearer to "the Greek conception of good citizenship than to the stoical austerity of recent verse" (1932). "Our goal which we compel: Man shall be man," declared Spender emphatically, in a line more charged with conviction than precision.

It is this vision of change, and the transvaluation of values it implies, that particularly demands the attention of Christian sensibilities. Out of the four poets thought of as a group — Auden, Spender, Day Lewis, MacNeice — only one, Auden, gave his later assent to the basic tenets of the Christian faith. In all of them however, to some extent, we witness the manifestation of Christian values and beatitudes dissociated from orthodox terminology. What we discover is a striving for grace in terms that fit neither a traditionally supernatural nor a conventionally rationalistic usage. And since in the most powerful poetry there is always a suggestion of revelation, what we find in the best work of these four is the sense of charisma in secular context. As MacNeice wrote in *An Eclogue for Christmas:*

> Goodbye to you, this day remember is Christmas, this morn
> They say, interpret it your own way, Christ is born.

A strange analogy

If we seek to date the birth of this movement, then Spender's hand-printing of an edition ("about thirty copies") of Auden's first volume entitled *Poems* in 1928 makes a convenient start. It also serves to spotlight Auden, who was the seminal mind of the group as well as being its impresario. On account of his larger status, Auden merits separate treatment in this series; but no summary of the Pylon poets can explain the nature or direction of their work without some preliminary reference to him. We have only to read Spender's autobiography *World within World,* or note the many references and dedications to him in the volumes of the Pylon poets, to see the influence he exerted.

From the Introduction that he wrote to *Oxford Poetry,* 1927, it is clear that Auden possessed a mind sharper and more subtle than most undergraduates. He disclaimed, straight away, any appeal to the teen-age cult which was rife in the post-War years. "Those," he wrote, "who believe that there is anything valuable in our youth as such, we have neither the patience to consider nor the power to condone: our youth should be a period of spiritual discipline." (Here one is reminded of the statement Eliot was to make a few years later in "Thoughts after Lambeth," namely that what the young need to be taught is "chastity, humility, austerity, and discipline." Auden and Eliot hold different ends in view, but both stress the necessity of self-ascesis as a means.)

Auden evidently exercised the ringmaster's function to the manner-born. "He had," Spender tells us, "the strangest sense of looking for colleagues and disciples . . . He looked at a still life on the wall and said: 'He will be the Painter . . . His friend Isherwood was to be the Novelist. Chalmers was another of the Gang. Cecil Day Lewis was a colleague. A group of emergent artists existed in his mind, like a cabinet in the mind of a party leader."

The spell of Auden — the shaman-like effect of his personality — is apparent from all that Spender recounts. "I took to showing Auden my poems," he confesses. "I would arrive with my pockets stuffed with manuscripts and watch him reading them. Occasionally he would grunt. Beyond this his comment was restrained to selecting one line for praise. I showed him a long poem, after reading which he said,

'In a new land shooting is necessary

is a beautiful line,' and immediately the line entered as it were his own poetic landscape of deserted mines, spies, shootings — terse syllables enclosed within a music like the wind in a deserted shaft."

Auden at Oxford made the deep impression he did because he appeared to know all the answers and because the answers he gave appeared new. "At this early age," Spender relates, "Auden had already an extensive knowledge of the theories of modern psychology, which he used as a means of understanding himself and dominating his friends." Largely speaking, these theories were of a Freudian nature, but the key one, or pet one, concerned the psychosomatic origins of illness. "In 1929," as Isherwood narrates, "during a visit to Berlin, he came into contact with the doctrines of the American psychologist Homer Lane . . . Auden was particularly interested in Lane's theories of the psychological causes of disease — if you refuse to make use of your creative powers, you grow a cancer, etc." — which is exactly what that poor spinster did in Auden's ballad of Miss Gee. Isherwood remarks how "references to these theories can be found in many of the early poems," and indeed in the early poems of his friends. Without knowledge of these theories — namely, "If you are sick, this merely means that your desires are urging you, through sickness, to do what you really want, not what you think you ought to" — it is well-nigh impossible to understand the import of such a phrase as "the liar's quinsy" in Auden's key poem "Sir, No Man's Enemy."

In this poem, the person of the Healer (suggested presumably by Lane) is identified with the God-figure and addressed as such:

> Sir, no man's enemy, forgiving all
> But will his negative inversion, be prodigal:
> Send us power and light, a sovereign touch
> Curing the intolerable neural itch . . .

The poem follows the petitionary structure of a prayer. (Note how the supplication "Harrow the house of the dead" suggests here Christ's harrowing of hell.)

The status that Freud and Lane occupy in the Pylon poets is analogous to that which Christ's ministry of healing occupies in the Gospel records. With the analysts as guides, these poets hoped to exercise, extend, and explore the therapeutic miracle.

It is important to stress the psychological aspect of their vision. For them, the revolution was first to be a personal and internal affair. Writing of the year 1928 at Oxford, MacNeice states that "neither Auden nor Spender had yet shown the slightest interest in politics and, with a few exceptions such as Clare Parsons [an undergraduate poet who died young], the cult of Soviet Russia was something almost unknown."

Isherwood endorses this by telling us that the creative revolt of these poets was not primarily political.

> The Angry Young Man of my generation was angry with the Family and its official representatives; he called them hypocrites, he challenged the truth of what they taught. He declared that a Freudian revolution had taken place of which they were trying to remain unaware. He accused them of reactionary dullness, snobbery, complacency, apathy. While they mouthed their platitudes, he exclaimed, we were all drifting towards mental disease, sex crime, alcoholism, suicide.

The activity of the young Pylon poets in their early years suggests a parallel with the first Christian communities: supporting and encouraging one another in a hostile world, and seeking, all the time, to carry over their conviction into that larger arena. There is the same cooperative effort: Auden and Isherwood combined to write their three verse-plays together (*The Dog Beneath the Skin*, 1935; *The Ascent of F6*, 1936; and *On the Frontier*, 1938), followed by their prose-verse account of a trip to China entitled *Journey to a War*, in 1939; Auden and MacNeice collaborated in *Letters from Iceland*, in 1936.

Then, too, there is the equivalent of the first Christians' certitude, their sense of uniquely possessing the Word, in what Peter Porter has called — while speaking of the last work — a sort of " 'in-group' knowingness." Another parallel presents itself in what might metaphorically be termed the chiliasm of the Pylon poets; for whereas the early Christians believed in a second coming of Christ as king of this world, so these poets believed in a passing away of the present order of things and the establishment of a more equitable community, a society in which "No one/Shall hunger: Man shall spend equally," a kingdom, in short, wherein "Man shall be man."

"No one shall hunger" ("Feed my flock") . . . "The palpable and obvious love of man for man" ("Love thy neighbor as thyself"). It was, then, ultimately the attempt of the Pylon poets to fulfill *both* of Christ's commands, external and internal, in purely secular terms, that sustains the parallel between them and the early adherents of the Faith. Finally, by an act of fancy, we see Auden cast in the role of St. Paul, exhorting, approving, condemning, casting out, and generally stage-managing the poetic revolution. "You came away from his presence always encouraged," MacNeice declared, recalling him at Oxford. It was certainly not without reason that Auden, in his *New Year Letter*, 1941, accused himself of having employed "the preacher's loose immodest tone"; nor should Isherwood's recollection of Auden's various hats, among which was included "a panama with a black ribbon — representing, I think, Auden's conception of himself as a lunatic clergy-man," be entirely discounted as evidence.

Perhaps there is something indicative too in the fact that Auden's parents were devoutly practicing Anglo-Catholics; that Day Lewis's father was a Church of Ireland vicar, and MacNeice's father a Church of Ireland bishop. In their late adolescent rebellion against the family and its values, could they have been driven to seek a father-figure, a savior-figure, a healer-figure elsewhere? "O descend," wrote Auden in his poem "Spain," ironically invoking the life-force, "O descend as a dove or / A furious papa or a mild engineer, but descend." The facetious tone and the irony need not imply the absence of emotional identification here.

In endeavoring to find a twin solution to man's economic and emotional needs, the poets were thinking along advanced contemporary lines. The two sage-figures in terms of which the writers of the thirties understood man's existence were Marx and Freud, two prophets not always reconcilable. Nothing possibly was more significant of the avant-garde's attempt to unify the culture of the times than the convenient synthesis effected by Osborne in his book *Freud and Marx*; and the work of the Pylon poets can be seen as an imaginative attempt to produce an equivalent synthesis. Indeed, their view of life might lead us to speak of their work in terms of Eros among the economists. As Spender wrote in "After they have tired":

> And our strength is now the strength of our bones
> Clean and equal like the shine from snow
> And the strength of famine and enforced idleness,
> And it is the strength of our love for each other.

II STEPHEN SPENDER

"Son of the puritan decadent"

Some slight knowledge of Spender's family background helps to make clear to the reader the direction in which his poetry moved.

Stephen Spender was born in London on February 28, 1909, the son of an ambitious but ineffectual political journalist. He was of partly German descent on his mother's side, and felt always a greater affinity with German than French literature, as, indeed, did Auden and Isherwood.

His high-minded parents brought him up in a too guarded way, trying to screen him from reality. There is a reflection of this in his poem "The Fates," which summarizes the price one pays for an upbringing that excludes the facts and removes the pain from reality. Here, it is the mother-figure who is censured:

> You were that painted mask of motherhood
> For twenty years, while you denied the real
> Was anything but the exceptional.

"Poverty, adultery, disease" — all these unfortunate undeniables were, for this good lady, monstrosities to be blinked away, conditions it was best to close one's eyes to:

> This is the stage where nothing happens that can matter
> Except that we look well-produced and bright.

One of the realities from which the young Spender was protected was the horseplay of poorer children. As a result of this, Spender with his compassionate, masochistic, and complex nature grew up to find a strange appealing glamor in the poor and unemployed.

There was certainly a strong sacrificial strain in his make-up; and he tells us how when young, "lying in bed, there were times when I regretted not having my arms extended on a cross with rusty nails driven through my hands."

In the first poem, about poor children, it is the sacrificial-masochistic urge that is obvious:

> They threw mud
> While I looked the other way, pretending to smile,
> I longed to forgive them, but they never smiled.

while in the second poem, about the unemployed, it is compassion that the poet mainly feels:

> I'm jealous of the weeping hours
> They stare through with such hungry eyes.
> I'm haunted by these images,
> I'm haunted by their emptiness.

The other factors in Spender's life that have a strong bearing on his poetry can be shortly related. After an early love affair in Vienna, he formed an attachment to a young man called Jimmy Younger who later joined the International Brigade, was wounded, deserted, and finally shot. Spender has described this friendship with great honesty in his autobiography. He was twice married: first in 1936 to Inez Holden, an Oxford student and eager Communist; then, in 1941, to the pianist Natasha Litvin (to whom his *Collected Poems*, 1945, were dedicated).

Another relationship important to the poet was that with his sister-in-law Margaret Spender, who died of cancer, after great suffering, on Christmas day 1945. Margaret was his confidante during those months when his first marriage was breaking up, and showed him, as he said, "a courage and hope which seemed the final development of a line through her fearless and happy life which even illness could not break." Spender commemorates her in a series of eight poems, *Elegy for Margaret*, written in 1945.

Little else in Spender's life is relative to his poetry. In World War II he served in the Auxiliary Fire Service, about which he has written amusingly in *World within World*. His experience of enforced communal life does not appear to have triggered the lyrical impulse associated with the idea of fraternity in his earlier poems. The London blitz, however, was responsible for one vivid apocalyptic poem, "Epilogue to a Human Drama" ("When pavements were blown up, exposing nerves,/ And the gas mains burned blue and gold").

For the rest, the chief landmarks of his existence have a professional rather than a poetic importance. For a while he helped Cyril Connolly edit the magazine *Horizon*, an important wartime meeting-ground for writers of all generations. After the war era he became editor of the more intellectualist journal *Encounter*; in 1965 he was appointed Consultant in Poetry to the Library of Congress at Washington.

"The most personal poet"

Of the four Pylon poets Spender's output in verse is the smallest. His *Collected Poems* (1954) contains fewer pages than those of the other members of the movement, and since that date he has also published little work in verse. What is important about his poetry is its sensibility, the quality of which we shall examine. A further distinction must also be made, in that the perception and feeling-tone of the poems is often in advance of their artistic success. Spender is an uneven poet, and many of his interesting poems, which hold us by reason of their sensitiveness or evident sincerity, fail to achieve full harmony of style or total unity of effect. One may, in fact, say that whereas Auden is the "idea man" of the group, Day Lewis its most instinctive artist, and MacNeice its brilliant verbal *tour-de-force* writer, Spender is the most *personal* poet. Auden's poems are fables and parables, Day Lewis's songs and *objets d'art,* MacNeice's are subtle analyses, and Spender's largely private confessions. Philip O'Connor has put this very well when he remarks that "critics, who now make a mystique of impersonality, have given up hope of the other, have sometimes affected amusement at his 'emotionality' (which requires actually a grinding impersonality to achieve in poetry). But this is precisely his courage and integrity." He also explains what lies behind the poet's unevenness and the curious "unprofessional" live interest of his verse — its "human document" hold upon the reader — when he suggests for

Spender's obituary: "He never rested in peace." "His anxiety," writes O'Connor, "was original, and he has never overcome it."

Of Spender's chief work in verse and prose, in addition to those already spoken of, mention must be made of *Nine Entertainments* (1928) published when he was only nineteen; *Twenty Poems* (1930); *Poems* (1933), which marked his first clear statement of political commitment; and *The Still Centre* (1939), published when he was still "preoccupied with various kinds of political activity" and "written directly and fairly quickly from the experiences which suggested them." Cyril Connolly has remarked how the poems in this volume on the Spanish Civil War are "far removed from his Communist enthusiasm of 1933"; and Spender himself has commented that the book contains a section of poems where "I have deliberately turned back to a kind of writing which is more personal, and . . . have included within my subjects weakness and fantasy and illusion." For many critics and readers *The Still Centre* is Spender's key volume. *Ruins and Visions* (1942) ended, remarks O'Connor, the poet's "flirtation with social reality, and reflected the 'blues' theme of our day, now also cracking up. Personal relations are asked to do the impossible: to stand in for a society that has failed the poet." Other books of verse include *Poems of Dedication* (1947) and *The Edge of Being* (1949).

His best criticism, as Kenneth Allott remarks, is contained in *The Destructive Element* (1935). The thesis of this book, rather over-simplified in MacNeice's words, is that Henry James, "like Proust [and other writers] was a herald of the Revolution; not being born at the right moment, all such writers could do was to immerse in the destructive element [James's phrase for the soul-destroying existence of a corrupt society]. But now the right moment had come." *The Destructive Element* was a subtle prolegomena to the pro-communistic *Forward from Liberalism* (1937). This acceptance of "Marxism as a working creed" was formally repudiated by Spender in *Life and the Poet* (1942), in which he declares that

> the ultimate aim of politics is not politics, but the activities which can be practised within the political framework of the state. Therefore an effective statement of these activities — such as science, art, religion — is in itself a declaration of ultimate aims around which political means will crystallize . . .
> A society with no values outside politics is a machine carrying its human cargo, with no purpose in its institutions reflecting their cares, eternal aspirations, loneliness, need for love.

This is Spender's fundamental declaration of a personalist position from which he has not substantially diverged. Other works of criticism are his monographs *Shelly* (1960) and *Poetry since 1939* (1946), *The Creative Element* (1953), and *The Making of a Poem* (1955).

"Only connect . . ."

All that is most positive in Spender's poetry would seem to spring from gestures of imaginative and emotional charity; and it is, of course, this aspect of his work that most engages the Christian critical mind. Against Spender's disposition of mind and his poems, which may be viewed as his "good works" (both being interpretable in a pan-Christian fashion), must be placed his rejection of belief and his repudiation of the church as an enemy of light and the forces of the new. Thus, in his poem "Landscape near an Aerodrome," the passengers in the arriving plane hear "the tolling bell" and see where, below them, "Religion stands, the church blocking the sun." Spender, intellectually, has proclaimed himself a sceptic, but defined his scepticism in an open and flexible way: "By scepticism," he told O'Connor, "I . . . mean scepticism about all dogmatic views. Atheism seems to me just as dogmatic as belief, and much narrower. Scepticism is quite consistent with respecting beliefs." Spender's scepticism, indeed, is of the sort that registers the emotional and imaginative impact of faith without that of its intellectual content. It is this which causes him to confess that he is "frightened by visions of belief, because with my kind of scepticism, any lot of believers may be right; I do not know anything to prove they are not right. For all I know, Hell is exactly as Dante described it . . . and Hell is something I certainly give a lot of thought to." Spender's position with regard to faith is therefore not an anti- but a non-relational one.

St. Paul, speaking of faith, hope, and charity, would seem to equate the workings of the first two with prophecy, preaching, and doctrine: "but whether *there be* prophecies, they shall fail; whether *there be* tongues, they shall cease; whether *there be* knowledge, it shall vanish away." Against the inadequacy of these two gifts ("now we see through a glass darkly"), St. Paul posits the perennial nature of the third: "Charity never faileth," being the greatest of these three. It is along some such line of thought that Spender may be reckoned a pan-Christian poet.

The critic Middleton Murry once described the First World War as a "defeat of the imagination" — a failure, namely, to identify ourselves with the conditions of others, since this would have made war unthinkable. E. M. Forster, likewise, has emphasized the same need for identification in his epigraph to *Howard's End*: "Only connect." It is the distinction of Spender as a poet that he almost invariably makes this connection of identification, particularly with those who, remote, alien, or even hostile, stand most in need of it. One sees this power of his to "connect" with others in poem after poem, in present terms, with the pupils in an elementary school classroom in a slum (where the future for these children is "painted with a fog / A narrow street sealed in with a lead sky, / For far from rivers, capes, and stars of words"); or in historical terms, with the exploited children of the nineteenth century, engaged in chimney-sweeping, factory labor, and work in mines ("You are the birds of a songless age / . . . You whisper among wheels / Calling to your stripped and sacred mothers / With straps tied round their waists / For dragging trucks along a line"). One finds it in certain poems on the English Civil War when he imagines how a mist, like "common suffering"

> Whitens the air with breath and makes both one
> As though these enemies slept in each other's arms.

It is easy to see how Spender could never have been a successful Communist Party poet. A Party man must *hate* the other side; whereas Spender's tendency is, always, to seek to understand and forgive. And when he does speak of hatred, it is seldom of a collective kind geared to a standard ideology, but something at once both personal and universal. Thus, in the same poem, when he describes two armies confronting each other, dug deep in the winter plain, he observes how

> All have become so nervous and so cold
> That each man hates the cause and distant words
> That brought him here, more terrible than bullets.
> Once a boy hummed a popular marching song;
> The voice was choked, the lifted hand fell
> Shot through the wrist by those of his own side.

One can imagine how such truths must have endeared

the poet to the literary commissars of the Left. Other poems of his expressing pity are "The Prisoners," "The Drowned," "The Coward" — all dealing with those types whom fate has cast as underdogs.

And when the subject of the poem is nearer to the poet himself, the charity increases. Such a poem is "Song," which treats of the break-up of his marriage and speaks of himself, his wife, and her lover. In it the charity is magnificently sustained because each party in the situation is granted a measure of justice. This is one of the great love poems of all time. Beside it, the wit and irony of Catullus and Donne are those of conceited playboys with the clever understanding of cock-sparrow. The charity in this poem is complex in the extreme. It cannot be equated with Christian forgiveness; it is rather a vision of justice, at an elemental psychological level — a justification of those facts and forces that give to each his identity.

One of the great exercises in charity found in Spender's verse is discoverable in his poem-sequence *Elegy for Margaret,* the composition that combines a description of his sister-in-law's inch-by-inch dying with a sensitive commemoration of her spirit. Here Spender seems to demonstrate that an act of the imagination, in such a context as this, is almost synonymous with an act of charity. Here, to observe is to self-identify:

> You are so quiet: your hand on the sheet seems a mouse
> Yet when we turn away, the flails
> That pound and beat you down with ceaseless pulse
> Shake like steam hammers through the house.

G. S. Fraser has noted Spender's sympathy with those who manifest "self-pity rather than stoicism, weakness rather than strength, failure rather than success." It should be remarked, however, that Spender's own self-pity is balanced always by a powerful self-knowledge which permits him no deception. In the splendid poem that speaks of the aftermath of his broken marriage, he ends with a statement of self-analysis tantamount to self-condemnation:

> At first you did not love enough
> And afterwards you loved too much
> And you lacked the confidence to choose
> And you have only yourself to blame.
> ("The Double Shame")

Spender's attitude of "humility about one's own weakness and charity for the weakness of others" sets him apart from his colleagues. When he writes that "An 'I' can never be a great man/.../ The great 'I' is an unfortunate intruder/ Quarrelling with 'I tiring' and 'I sleeping'/And all those other I's who long for 'We dying'," he is, by implication, criticizing the sin of pride and presenting the human image scaled down to a sense of mortal limitation. Spender appears to see man in terms of Original Sin — Original Sin operating without God.

In the poet's scheme of things, love takes the place of deity, though he is careful to allot it no omnipotent power. As has been said, part of Spender's originality lay in his thinking of *eros* as *agape*. He envisaged libidinal self-fulfilment in terms of the love-feast of brothers, cameraderie and intimacy between all men, and a personal care and concern for their condition.

It was during his early years in Germany that he developed these notions. This personal liberation of his repressions took place within a landscape of political revolution.

> Christopher [Isherwood] and I, leading our life in which we used Germany as a kind of cure for our personal problems, became even more aware that the care-free personal lives of our friends were facades in the front of the immense social chaos. There was more and more a feeling that this life would be swept away. When we were on holiday at Insel Ruegen, where the naked bathers in their hundreds lay stretched on the beach under the drugging sun, sometimes we heard orders rapped out, and even shots, from the forest whose edges skirted the shore, where the Storm Troopers were training like executioners waiting to martyr the naked and self-disarmed.

The political timing of these activities synchronized, then, with the timing of Spender's own private emancipation; and just as he reacted against the extreme erotic license of the German libertarians to work out his own idea of love, so he reacted against the antihumanitarian Nazism to develop his own notion of a personalist socialism.

Sometimes Spender writes, in a personal poem, of the therapeutic value of *eros:*

> My healing fills the night
> And hangs its flags in worlds I cannot near.
> Our movements range through miles, and when we kiss
> The moment widens to enclose the years.

At other times, it is not love received but love projected that offers the solution. Thus, in his poem on a deserted spot in the Spanish War, he concludes with these sentiments:

> Nothing can count but love, to pour
> Out its useless comfort here.
> To populate his loneliness
> And to bring his ghost release
> Love and pity dare not cease
> For a lifetime, at the least.

Speaking of Whitman, in one of his excellent Introductions to *Poets of the English Language,* Auden characterizes three distinctive attitudes to the body: the pagan, the puritan, and the liberal-idealistic. This third point of view regards the body as a nuisance, an irrelevance, something that impedes the "real" activities of life which take place in the mind or the spirit. Spender's experience in Germany, and the poetry he made out of it, rectify this transcendental imbalance. Both in his poetry of love and in his socialist poetry, he stresses the *relevance* of the body — something that gives the "real" activities of mind and spirit a proper context. Spender, of course, had himself been brought up in a family atmosphere where the body was regarded, at the best, as troublesome; at the worst, as unclean. The figure of the son in his poem "The Fates" conveys this censorship of the *superego:*

> And yet he had his moments of uneasiness
> When, in the dazzling garden of his family,
> With green sunlight reflected on your dress,
> His body suddenly seemed an obscenity,
> A changeling smuggled to the wrong address.

It is, of course, the mother — with her rejection of the physical — who makes the son uneasy (note, too, how the mother's personality is presented in terms of "sunlight" and "dress," i.e. unearthy and inanimate elements, while the son's is presented in terms of "His body" as if, seen through her eyes, he was nothing but the carnal part of his make-up).

The distance between the imprisonment of the body in the first poem and its liberation, both personally and collectively, in the compostition "O young men oh young comrades" is enormous. A whole internal revolution in the poet's nature has taken place, something that required as catalytic agents German nudism, hitchhiking, and free love. Against the inheritance of money and property, the poet tells the young men to

> Count rather those fabulous possessions
> which begin with your body and your fiery soul:
> the hairs on your head the muscles extending

> in ranges with lakes across your limbs.
> Count your eyes as jewels and your valued sex
> then count the sun and the innumerable coined light
> sparkling in waves and spangling under trees.

In the last three lines of the above passage, we see Spender reintegrating man with nature (viewed as his proper habitation) as distinct from the urban landscape of an acquisitive society:

> it is too late now to stay in those houses
> your fathers built where they built you to breed
> money on money.

Instead, the young men are exhorted to "step beautifully from the solid wall/ advance to rebuild and sleep with friend on hill/ advance to rebel." Here, in what might be called a radical democracy of touch, the erotic and the political are closely associated.

In this poem, as elsewhere, Spender envisages socialism in clearly physical terms. There is much of Whitman's fraternalism in it; but in Spender's case the brotherly feelings imply a "brotherly politic" while Whitman's moments of brotherly nearness are isolated within a politic of cutthroat competitive individualism. The American poet's social optimism seems to us now a lapse of intelligence.

Everywhere, in speaking of love and socialism, Spender seeks to present an organic image — a physical objective correlative, which shall express the actual or potential concrete living of the situation. Thus, we have metaphors from botany or animal biology to represent the nascent life of revolutionary sensibility. The "comrades" who have "tired of the brilliance of cities," "the failure of banks," and "the failure of cathedrals" (urban inanimate imagery) are exhorted not to lack "the spring-like resources of the tiger/ Or of plants which strike out new roots to urgent waters."

Spender's large avoidance of the abstract, with which Marxist thought is overloaded, gave to his poetry an immediate appeal all too rare in Communist poets. He leaves a clear visual impression when he speaks about one particular moment in history — the interbellum peace in 1929 before Hitler's coming to power —

> A whim of time, the general arbiter,
> Proclaims the love, instead of death, of friends.
> Under the doomed sky and athletic sun
> Three stand naked: the new bronzed German,
> The communist clerk, and myself, being English.

This stands in interesting contrast to the Marxist poet John Cornford's "Full Moon at Tierz: Before the Storming of Huesca":

> The past, a glacier, gripped the mountain wall,
> And time was inches, dark was all.
> But here it scales the end of the range,
> The dialectic's point of change,
> Crashes in light and minutes to its fall.

Without the title to inform us, we should not know what Cornford referred to. There is no setting of the scene; and whereas, with Spender's passage, the abstract noun "time" is soon given "local habitation and a name," here it is integrated in a web of other abstract terms: time, inches, dialectic, minutes. It is, of course, the word "dialectic" that obfuscates the whole passage. In the same poem, Cornford tells us that "with my Party, I stand quite alone"; and his statement explains the failure of his language. He has used Party-speech, the connotations of which have no common usage. Unless we are read in historical materialism, the term "dialectic" here is all but meaningless. It is Spender's distinction that, surrendering for a while, in part, to a philosophy alien to his nature, he preserved his own speech. Unless a poet's tongue is his own, he is little better than a hack.

The final remark remains to be made about Spender's revolutionary verse, namely, the sense of limitation that the poet speaks about at work in the Utopias and their millennial program:

> What I had not foreseen
> Was the gradual day
> Weakening the will
> Leaking the brightness away,
> The lack of good to touch,
> The fading of body and soul
> — Smoke before wind,
> Corrupt, unsubstantial.

One could have no finer summing up of man's natural bias to defection, as implied by Original Sin, than this.

"A sensitive agnostic"

If Spender's poetry lacks wit, it is certainly, like Falstaff, the cause of wit in others. Sometimes, as in the description of him as "the Rupert Brooke of the depression," it is little more than a malicious half-truth (though Cyril Connolly's statement that "Spender's early poetry was characterized by an inspired innocence" should not be forgotten here). Francis Scarfe's phrase for him — "the Wilfred Owen of the Peace" — certainly comes much nearer the mark, though Scarfe himself felt it was not adequate to represent Spender's attitude, finding in the poet "far more than a negation" and "the clamorous pitiful protest of Owen." (Again, however, one should remember that for Spender, as for the War poet, clearly "the poetry is in the pity.")

Little has been written on the nature and quality of his language, though Francis Scarfe in *Auden and After* and G. S. Fraser in *Vision and Rhetoric* both have excellent essays on him. MacNeice once described him as a poet patiently pressing clichés into poetic shape with steady and powerful hands. This is not the destructive epigram it seems. Spender is too prone to poeticisms, to frilly and tinselly speech, or to its converse, flat, awkward diction. Sometimes this is evidently due to the boring necessity of the subject (a matter of the poet's expending his powers "on the flat ephemeral pamphlet" or some such political homily). Scarfe, indeed, notices how "the lyrical passages in Spender's propagandist poems occur largely as reactions against what he is preaching," while Fraser remarks that "The typical quality of his style, arising from [a] paradoxical combination of a desire 'to let himself go' and a fear 'of letting himself go' is a stumbling eloquence or a sweeping gesture suddenly arrested."

Verbally and temperamentally, poets may obviously be divided into soft-and hard-center types. Spender is distinctly a soft-center poet just as Auden is a hard. These epithets do not imply value-judgments: they merely suggest the oper-ation of two distinct modes of sensibility. In this context it seems appropriate to comment on Thom Gunn's notorious attack on Spender in his *Lines to a Book,* since it assumes soft-center sensibility to be intrinsically valueless and also distorts Spender's text. "I think," writes Gunn,

> of all the toughs through history
> And thank heaven they lived continually.
> I praise the overdogs from Alexander
> To those who would not play with Stephen Spender.

The reference, of course, is to Spender's poem which begins

"My parents kept me from children who were rough," implying that it was the poet who was *not allowed* to play with rough children and not the children who *would not* play with the poet. Gunn's poem, by the way, is as nice a compendium of nasty virtues as one could easily come by — a version of Nietzsche as a leather-jacket boy.

Only one critic, so far as I know, considers Spender the superior of Auden. The latter's (sometimes showy) brilliance with words and ideas is so disarming that we forget· that poetry is something besides an intellectual conjuring act plus a verbal *tour de force*. That something is, of course, the property on which Spender's backers must stake their claim.

Scarfe describes the poet's basic theme when he writes that "Spender has his own drama: a struggle to adapt his individualism to his social views, and a struggle to understand and perfect his individuality." O'Connor sees Spender as suffering from the personification of a social ailment, "more so than Auden making him, in my opinion, a more important poet — more representative, more articulately sensitive."

This last opinion brings once more into focus the sacrificial scapegoat element in Spender, so that when G. S. Fraser describes the poet as "a sensitive agnostic, whose soul indeed might be described as naturally religious or even *naturaliter Christiana*," we readily assent.

III Louis MacNeice

"A horse might shy"

The outward facts of Louis MacNeice's life are quickly told. He was born in Belfast on September 12, 1907, son of a Protestant archdeacon, later to become Bishop of Down. He took a first at Merton College, Oxford — the only one of the Pylon poets to secure initial academic distinction.

He was married on Midsummer Day 1929 in a register office in Carfax, to a girl he met at Oxford, who came of a wealthy Levantine family, after having first staggered his father (who "had a horror of drink") by wiring him to the effect that he had been put in jail for drunkenness and was engaged to marry a Jewess.

From 1930 to 1936 he was Lecturer in Classics at Birmingham, then became Lecturer at Bedford College, a women's college which is part of the University of London. In 1935, a year after the birth of a daughter, MacNeice and his wife separated and were later divorced.

Settling in London, near Primrose Hill, MacNeice wrote two travel books, one in verse and one in prose. The first of these, *Letters from Iceland* (1937), was a joint production with Auden, following the two poets' trip to that country. The second, entitled *I Crossed the Minch* (1938), is a volume of Irish impressions in prose.

During this period he also wrote two works of criticism: *Modern Poetry* (1938) and *W. B. Yeats* (1941), "for which I had no vocation but which I thought to myself, I could do as well as the next man." He visited America in 1939, and was Lecturer in Poetry at Cornell University in the first part of 1940. Returning to England in war time, he was employed by the B.B.C. from 1941-9, engaged in the writing and producing of plays and features. He had already translated *The Agamemnon of Aeschylus* (1936), and this was followed by a series of broadcast dramas: *Out of the Picture, The Mad Island, The Administrator,* and *Christopher Colombus,* published together under the title *The Dark Tower and Other Radio Scripts* (1947). In 1951, he published a version of Goethe's *Faust.*

1950 saw him made a director of the British Institute at Athens, and he continued writing and publishing verse until his untimely death in September 1963. Two volumes appeared posthumously: a book of verse, *The Burning Perch* (1963), and an unfinished autobiography, *The Strings Are False* (1965), which he had written early in the war and then placed, unrevised, in a friend's safekeeping.

"A Kingdom without a King"

Much, no doubt, of MacNeice's nature, and possibly the greater part of his pose, is to be explained by the familiar pattern of the only son's rebellion against the family gods. And as these family gods were the figures of the Trinity, understood in terms of Low Church theology according to the worship of the Church of Ireland, and as the poet's father was a dignitary of that institution — albeit a provincial dignitary — MacNeice's attitude to formal Christianity was negatively crytallized from the start.

Not that MacNeice could escape a sense of guilt. His early "Intimations of Mortality" (with obvious ironic reference to Wordsworth) recreates the poet in his nursery days, feeling his projections of the spiritual world impinge in nightmare fashion:

> He is afraid of God and the Devil.
> If he shuts his eyes they will draw level,
> So he watches the half-open door and waits
> For people on the stairs carrying lights.

But at length the whole household sleeps, and then the supernatural powers will claim him:

> After one perfunctory kiss
> His parents snore in conjugal bliss.
> The nightwatchman with crossed thumbs
> Grows an idol. The Kingdom comes . . .

For a while, at Marlborough, MacNeice proclaimed he was going to be a missionary; and one of his earliest pieces, entitled *The Creditor*, presents the poet attempting to lull himself

> In quiet in diet in riot in dreams
> In dopes in draws in drums in dreams
> Till God retire and the door shut.

Yet for all MacNeice's contrived escapism (a cult which the poet maintained throughout his life, but which never proved successful because of his powerful analytic intellect, ready to "rip the edge off any ideal or dream"), he still feels his "debt to God" unrescinded.

The Christian doctrine, in the family context and the context of his home town Carrickfergus, seems to have been associated by the poet with all that was negative and unlovely. "The human elements of this world," he writes in *Landscapes of Childhood and Youth*, "need not be detailed: guilt, hell fire, Good Friday, the doctor's cough, hurried lamps in the night, melancholia, mongolism, violent sectarian voices. All this sadness and conflict and attrition and frustration were set in this one acre near the smoky town within sound not only of the tolling bell, but of the smithy that seemed to deny it."

MacNeice remarks that at Marlborough "most sons of clergymen . . . became would-be fast" — a gesture or pose of revolt or independence. At seventeen the poet shared a study with a boy who retained his family's puritanical tradition, and a "secret antipathy blossomed between them. Being with Ricketts," he wrote, "was like being with my family and what was forgivable in them seemed intolerably priggish in Ricketts." The sense of burden and ennui, and beneath it all the affection for his parents, is implicit in this statement. His sister, speaking of him after his death, commented on how he had seemed to change after his first three months at Marlborough, "becoming withdrawn as far as family communication was concerned." An early, uneasy, and wry, ironic poem, with the title "Happy Families," describes the enforced coziness of a young man pent up in the home circle:

> The room is all a stupid quietness,
> Cajoled only by the fire's covers;
> We loll severally about and sit
> Severally and do our business severally,
> For there's a little bit for everybody;
> But that's not all there is to it.

Behind the young MacNeice's rebellion, there lay, as Professor Dodds tell us, "a real strength and warmth of . . . feeling for his father, deeper than all surface irritations." It seems that he deferred the completion of his autobiography so that it should not occur during his father's lifetime. Two years after his father's death he published in his book of poems *Springboard,* section VII of his poem "The Kingdom," containing a generous tribute to his parent. His understanding of his father was indeed a clue to the poet of the "otherness" of all fellowmen, an "otherness" that implied not "alien-ness" but uniqueness:

> Under the surface of flux and of fear there is an underground movement,
> Under the crust of bureaucracy, quiet behind the posters,
> Unconscious but palpably there — the kingdom of individuals.

In the second verse-paragraph, the Christian echoes sound more distinctly:

> And of these is the Kingdom —
> Equal in difference, interchangeably, sovereign —

Christ told us to love our neighbor as ourselves; but love, to be operative, must recognize the rock of difference. Yet it is this resistant difference that proves, in its paradoxical fashion, the unrepeatable workmanship expended by the Creator on each person. That which demonstrates most clearly that God made man neither parrot nor machine, makes it also the more difficult for him to carry out Christ's injunction and love this *difference* as he loves himself.

From the third paragraph of the poem, it is clear that MacNeice understood the relational implications of this notion; namely, that a *community of caritas* can never be a social barracks of segregated living — a "community of mere convenience" for the separate lonely dwellers in their "little boxes." The members of this Kingdom in their mutual balance are described by the poet as follows:

> These, as being themselves, are apart from not each other
> But from such as being false are merely other,
> So these are apart as parts within a pattern
> Not merged nor yet excluded, members of a Kingdom
> Which has no King except each subject . . .

MacNeice's divergence from Christian thinking — *a Kingdom without a King* — is apparent in the last line. This is a point of differentiation that he is most emphatic about. He insists that the members of *his Kingdom* are to be thought of

> Apart from the easy religion of him who would find in God
> A boss, a ponce, an alibi, and apart from
> The logic of him who abrogates to himself
> The secret of the universe . . . .

Conceivably, the Christian might reply that neither is he looking in God for a boss, etc.; yet it is clear from the poet's tone and from his contemptuous dismissal of a revealed plan of the world, that MacNeice is repudiating the center and source of authority upon which Christianity stands. In many ways, however, this is his most positive poem and the nearest he was ever to come to thinking in pan-Christian terms.

"The Kingdom" remains something of an exception in MacNeice's work; and some of the factors that prevented him from developing the Christian note in his way may now be considered.

Chief of these, perhaps, was aestheticism: an attitude developed by MacNeice as a gesture of revolt but which also corresponded with something indigenous to his temperament, so that it became his living and thinking pattern. Sir Anthony Blunt, the art-historian, who was with the poet at school, has spoken of his intense visual sensibility and how he would stop in the street at Marlborough to watch, say, some scarlet-painted agricultural machinery driven on a hauler through the town. Poem after poem bears out this emotional responsiveness to color as the object not only of optical experience but as the stimulator of atmosphere and moods. Now it so happened that the associational elements of Christianity in the poet's family circle all appeared to him as drab and colorless. The philosopher Kierkegaard once defined the aesthetic attitude to life as belonging to the category of "the interesting" — not whether a thing was good or true, but whether it was piquant, attractive, intriguing. For the poet's family, this factor was, at the best, of secondary consideration. MacNeice's father "had played with the idea of sending [him] to Glasgow University, as being both more moral and industrious than Oxford." The poet, however, was wily enough to out-maneuver this suggestion. "I got my Oxford scholarship," he tells us, "almost before he realized I was entering for it ... I wrote home, however, to deprecate this performance and to explain that I saw through Oxford completely." To MacNeice, of course, it was unthinkable that Oxford with its status and style should be sacrificed for an ethical utilitarian choice. Another factor related to the poet's aestheticism was his social snobbery, though it was a snobbery based more on notions of taste than class. Merely being modish and "advanced" was an established principle of MacNeice at Marlborough and Oxford.

> I used to get up very late and cut my lectures, because the lecturers were inaudible or dull. I hated my tutorials — the endless interpolation into Greek composition of phrases carefully collected from writers of the proper period; I thought that was a game for the "monsters", i.e. the grammar school boys, those distorted little creatures with black teeth who held their forks by the middle and were set on making a career. I used to sit wedged between these monsters at dinner, listening superciliously as they discussed Noel Coward and Bernard Shaw; in my opinion no one intelligent would mention such writers.

MacNeice's "aesthetic hedonism" sprang from an intelligence naturally sceptical and a temperament innately elegiac and despairing. Nothing in his poetry is more surprising than the fund of imagery, the wealth of words, the sensuous vividness of texture, expended on what is finally, in most cases, a negative point of view.

At Oxford, he recalled, "Apart from my instincts I was now almost without principles. For example, if I felt sorry for people, I might be ready to do them a good turn, but I would have vigorously denied that there was anything morally good in this good turn. So-called altruism was merely a projection of egotism. On this base it was hard to choose — unless one's appetites came into it — between one course of action and another; it meant weighing one's ultimate self-interest and that was a bore." He confesses that he handed over the decision of choice to artistic caprice and intuition: "When in doubt I used to play over and over to myself a gramophone record — the Rondo of Mozart's E flat Horn Concerto — and then do what came into my head." One is reminded of Emerson, writing up the word "Whim" above his study door.

Nor were the aestheticians — any more than the metaphysicians — able to assist him here; he regarded philosophy as "an artistic account not a scientific one." This did not mean that he regarded philosophy as purposeless. "The philosopher's job," he declared, "— to use our favourite word — was stylisation, building a symphony which should sanction his emotional reactions to the universe. When you boil them down they are all alike." Philosophers, in other words, are to be assessed in terms of their degree of original pattern-making. Their category is that of "the interesting." They are coiners of artistic similes, not of statements of truth which, outside the realm of fact, he regarded as unknowable. It would, one supposes, be correct to think of MacNeice's intellectual attitude as one of sceptical pragmatism. The existence of things had to be posited "as if" they were authentic so that the business of living could proceed. But a vision of existence without ultimates or absolutes limits one's thinking to short-term decisions. One must sail the waves of phenomena, tacking with every pluralistic wind.

No doubt it was this predominating sense of the variability· of events that prevented him ever from sharing with the other Pylon poets the enthusiasm for Communism, with its rigidly doctrinaire thinking. It is instructive to compare Day Lewis's poem "Why, seeing a Communist, do we feel small?" with MacNeice's lines "To a Communist":

> Your thoughts make shapes like snow; in one night only
> The gawky earth grows breasts,
> Snow's unity engrosses
> Particular pettiness of stones and grasses.
> But before you proclaim the millenium, my dear,
> Consult the barometer —
> This poise is perfect but maintained
> For one day only.

Using his ever nimble visual imagination, the poet interprets the Marxian dialectic as giving, like snow to the earth, an appearance of uniformity. But this unity is of a specious order. Remove the theatrical blueprint of the future, and the old variability of history will once again be evident, just as the earth reveals its variety when the snow melts away from its surface.

Among the Pylon poets, MacNeice was always an odd man out. Because of their whilom pro-Communism, Auden, Spender, and Day Lewis were commonly referred to as "the Pink Triumvirate," whereas the most that could be said of MacNeice is that — in G. S. Fraser's phrase — he was "a left of center Liberal."

MacNeice's sceptism concerning the progressivist politic of Communism was matched by an equal doubt concerning the "advances" of avant-garde art. The aesthete in him was qualified by a large dose of common sense which rebelled at the way in which modern art had distorted the image of man. No modernist poem offers a more brilliant critique of the shifting mirror of contemporary art than MacNeice's "An Eclogue for Christmas":

> I who was Harlequin in the childhood of the century,
> Posed by Picasso beside an endless opaque sea,
> Have seen myself sifted and splintered in broken facets,
> Tentative pencilling, endless liabilities, no assets,
> Abstractions scalpelled with a paper knife
> Without reference to this particular life.
> And so it has gone on; I have not been allowed to be
> Myself in flesh or face, but abstracting and dissecting me
> They have made of me pure form, a symbol or a pastiche,
> Stylised profile, anything but soul and flesh.

MacNeice's rejection of the Procrustean bed upon which avant-garde art and progressivist politics stretch the image of man is a resistance to heresy in its two most significant contemporary manifestations. The Christian believes that man possesses a God-given nature and figure, able by a sort of parallel telepathy to communicate with his Creator. MacNeice believed that the individual — "myself in flesh or face" is the only guarantee of uniqueness. Both attitudes, in their different fashion, insist upon "the holy fact" — Charles Williams's phrase for the objective undeniable "given-ness" of things.

The social and political progressivism of the Pylon poets had never been embraced by MacNeice; and here one has a paradox, for none of the others can show so coruscating a modern surface imagery as MacNeice. Regarded in terms of its reference and imagery, his "Bagpipe Music" was probably the most topical poem of the whole thirties. Yet fascinated as MacNeice was by the virtuoso gimmickry of modern living, he never for one moment succumbs to a vague utopian hope. Indeed, the pieces in his last book, *The Burning Perch*, write off the future of the space age (which is also the age of the Welfare State) with wry contempt:

> In lieu therefore of choice
> Thy will be undone just as the flowers,
> Fugues, vows and hopes are undone
> While the weather is packaged and the spaceman
> In endless orbit and in lieu of a flag
> The orator hangs himself from the flagpost.

Nothing could be more advisedly bleak than his prospect of the technocrats' full-coverage society, ironically entitled "New Jerusalem." As he observes elsewhere, to attempt to live with "appetitive decorum" in an age when "quality has long been in pawn to security" is no inviting matter.

From the evidence of MacNeice's last book of verse alone, it is clear he died an unhappy man. The provisional pleasure-cult which he elaborated when young yielded, as needs be, fewer returns. Speaking of Paul Valery, T. S. Eliot once remarked that there were certain men of powerful intellects equipped with a built-in force of disbelief. This inability to believe is sometimes found in inverse proportion to the analytical powers of the mind; and when these factors combine with a temper constitutionally inclined to the negative, then only the grace of God can change things. One imagines MacNeice was just such a man.

The final flavor left by his last book is shrewd, wry, and tired. John Wain has spoken of "the *penchant* for a surface 'realism' characterising . . . MacNeice's poetry" up to and including *Autumn Journal* (1939). This *does*, no doubt, describe the outside skin of the poems. G. S. Fraser has commented on the "sensualist" element in MacNeice's verse, leading him to make "precise catalogues of sensation":

> Euston, the smell of soot and fish and petrol.

Fraser notes also that "his poetic attitude was that of the tough, learned, and witty Epicurian, shocked by the political wickedness and folly of the world into a proud contempt." Reinforcing this, as it were, Francis Scarfe thinks of him as a new-Augustan, "a neo-Dryden" — a poet of urbanity, wit, and common sense.

All these judgments hold one aspect of the truth; but reading through MacNeice's work in toto with his autobiography as a valuable gloss, it seems that these were attitudes — masks behind which the real man hid his face. The "real man" one might describe as a romantic — hungry for something fuller and finer than mundane living can generally offer — a poet of intensity posing in the role of a poet of balance. So, at least, one may construe the sixth of his epigraph pieces serially entitled *As in their Time*:

> He had clowned it through. Being born
> For either the heights or the depths
> He had bowled his hoop on the level
> Arena; the hoop was a wheel
> Of fire but he clowned it through.

Variety and contradictoriness

MacNeice's stylistic gift as a poet is readily stated: a versatile virtuosity extending from his first volume — "a book of juvenile poems" — *Blind Fireworks* (1929) to his last posthumous publication, *The Burning Perch* (1963). The best brief summary of his work is that made by Kenneth Allott.

> MacNeice's virtues include a fine sense of color, a satirical and observant eye, and a lively interest in words, rhymes, and rhythms. All his collections contain good poems. The variety of this goodness is to be noted: he has written excellent love-poetry, successful dramatic lyrics or character-sketches like the "Novelettes" of *Plant and Phantom* (1941), humorous and satirical verse like "Bagpipe Music," argumentative and reflective poetry like "Plurality." He can celebrate the ordinary and the everyday without putting his tongue in his cheek, because the imperviousness — except in time of war — of the ordinary man to politics, creeds, and -isms strikes a sympathetic cord in MacNeice .... His best work was unequalled in the 'thirties for its gaiety, grace, and a lightness which was never really silly or ostrich-like.

Insofar as poetry contributes to the culture of thought, or more accurately, to the current of ideas, MacNeice occupies no unimportant place. Comparing two passages from Eliot's "Dry Salvages" with a passage from MacNeice's "Plurality," Francis Scarfe sees the poet as occupied with a metaphysical problem, namely "the relation of human life to time." His poem, "Snow," deals with the "contradictoriness" of phenomenal happenings, "the drunkenness of things being various." This, like Robert Graves' "Waving to Children," is a classic statement of pluralistic poetry — of verse, in the latter poet's words, that sets out to convey a sense

> Of the greatness, rareness, muchness,
> Fewness of this precious only
> Endless world in which you say
> You live . . . .

If, in these few lines, Graves presents with admirable succinctness the infinite economy to be investigated, it is MacNeice who successfully translates this kind of world-awareness into terms of sensuous and elegant precision:

> The room was suddenly rich and the great bay-window was
> Spawning snow and pink roses against it
> Soundlessly collated and incompatible:
> World was suddener than we fancy it.

As a thinker, MacNeice is fascinated with the essential dilemmas of man as a creature subject to time and space. Early interested in Heraclitus, he examines the realms of space and time as constituting variety and flux. And if man's life in these dimensions is something to be endured or enjoyed rather than utterly reformed, this is because MacNeice believed that "things are not otherwise but thus." Here, it is of interest to compare him with W. H. Auden, a poet given to generalizing reflection even more inveterately than MacNeice. The difference between them is that all of Auden's thought belongs to the sphere of moral philosophy whereas that of MacNeice mostly deals with epistemology and metaphysics (the problems of knowing and being). That these problems are being undertaken by a pragmatic intelligence, given to regarding all things as "fragmented" and to thinking "in broken images," only makes the issue more piquant. To adopt the poet's own criteria, we know that the answers he offers can only be taken as relativistic, personal, and provisional. Auden, on the other hand, belongs to the same camp as Karl Marx, who said that "hitherto it had been the business of philosophers to explore and examine the world whereas now it was their job to change it." This means that a concept of thought in Auden, dealing with the problems of natural philosophy, is ultimately propaganda: a new way of stating a *thought*, so that fitting *action* may more easily follow. And if it is argued that the propagandist thinker must necessarily be revolutionary and that Auden, as we know, has passed beyond his revolutionary phase, then the answer is that with this poet all generalising thought (which is also propaganda) is intended to serve a therapeutic purpose. If we cannot always act to save ourselves, then perhaps we can put ourselves in a condition in which God can act upon us. It is in this sense, a modern rather than a classical one, that Auden is not a tragic poet; and MacNeice, with his sense of man's existence as conditioned by factors "beyond good and evil," just occasionally is.

The degree in which MacNeice's poetry conforms to Christian values is of importance, though small. Kierkegaard sought to establish the connection between the man who lives according to the category of "the interesting" (i.e. the aesthetic) and the man who lives in a state of despair. According to him, the man who lives according to the former precept, lives or will live in a state of despair, whether or not he is conscious of it. With his life-long (if modified) aestheticism, MacNeice appears as such a man; and poem after poem by him are, in fact, resonant with a despairing music. Yet, according to Christian canons, despair constitutes a cardinal sin, since in its fullest operation it negates not only the saving power of God but the relieving power of man through good works, particularly those of faith, hope, and charity.

If MacNeice's poetry offends against Christian values here, it does so in company with perhaps a good half of avant-garde writing. At the same time, this poetry offers, in one particular section of *Autumn Journal* (1939), a memorable manifestation of fortitude. Fortitude, of course, is one of the seven virtues referred to in the Anglican catechism, though it is one of Plato's four cardinal virtues rather than one of the three theological or supernatural virtues.

Since this section (II) of the poem argues, in experiential terms, the case for and against suicide — one of the key questions springing from contemporary literature's sense of "the absurd" — its importance can hardly be magnified. In this passage MacNeice presents us with a pitched battle between the death-wish and perseverance (perhaps what Santayana would call "animal faith"). The section begins with the image of a spider (as representing innate persistence) spinning, against all opposition and impediment, and despite repeated failure, his web of continuity. The poet has lost his love, and Europe teeters on the brink of war. All hopes for man, and himself, desert him:

> Glory to God in the Lowest, peace beneath the earth,
>> Dumb and deaf at the nadir;
> I wonder now whether anything is worth
>> The eyelid opening and the mind recalling.

As the poet looks over the log of the human story, no promise of hope by philosophy or religion appears to him as valid and substantial; and "the scent grows warm / For pure Non-Being, Nirvana." Yet, ultimately what holds him back is a sense of humility in the face of the "human animal's endless courage":

> Who am I — or I — to demand oblivion?
> I must go out tomorrow as the others do
> And build the falling castle.

Cyril Connolly sees *Autumn Journal* as completely seizing "the atmosphere of the year of Munich." Like David Gascoyne's poem "The Thirties" (set in Paris as distinct from MacNeice's London), it is one of those poems that toll the knell for a decade: reading it one senses the poet knew that history would never be the same again.

Probably his most positive poem — certainly, in a sense, his *credo* — is *Prayer before Birth*: a plea for the preservation of self-identity; a petition against the distorting or warping of the essential "I" by the harsh "otherness" of the world. The poem gathers force through a series of lengthening verse-paragraphs, then ends abruptly with a brisk either/ or:

> Let them not make me a stone and let them not spill me.
> Otherwise kill me.

In view of MacNeice's declared belief in the flux and plurality of existence, his assertion of personality in this poem as the one and indivisible *sine qua non* represents the sceptic's moral triumph over the germ of indifferentism within:

> Anchovies almond ice and gin
> All shall die though none can win;
> Let the Untergang begin —

"An Horatian poet haunted by the Void"

MacNeice's *Collected Poems* (1949) offers a representative bulk of his work. Section VII of this volume proclaims the change from a hedonist to a purposive technique. The

dedicatory poem "To Hedli" attempts to formulate the
poet's new intention:

> Because the velvet image,
> Because the lilting measure,
> No more conveys my meaning
> I am compelled to use
> Such words as disabuse
> My mind of carnal pleasure
> And turn it towards a centre
> A zone which others too
> And you
> May choose to enter.

It is doubtful, however, whether this change implies a
gain in *quality*. Broader, more ambitious, more extensive and
far-ranging the later poems certainly become. But *Autumn
Sequence* (1954) (written for broadcasting) gave the critic
G. S. Fraser "the sense that a fine pleasure was forcing
itself." The same critic noted, however, that in *Visitations*
(1957) the poet "seemed to have got back for the first
time in ten years or so the bite that he had had in the 1930's;
and in which he got away also from the snare of the
blown-up, big poem, of a length suitable for broadcasting."

With *Visitations,* the lyrical side of MacNeice's talent
(he had, commented T. S. Eliot, "the Irishman's unfailing
ear for the music of verse") seemed to experience a rebirth. The long poems he had written in *Ten Burnt
Offerings* (1951) and *Autumn Sequel* seemed to have caused,
as the poet remarked, "certain changes in my lyric writing"
"when the lyric impulse did return." "I like to think,"
noted MacNeice, "that my latest short poems are on the
whole more concentrated and better organised than the
earlier ones, relying more on syntax and on bony features
than on bloom or frill or floating image." The two volumes
following *Visitations* — *Solstices* (1961) and *The Burning
Perch* (1963), — amply fulfill the poet's supposition. Cyril
Connolly is not alone in believing this last volume to be
MacNeice's finest single selection. The Augustan poet of
common sense and reason, whom Francis Scarfe had seen
in MacNeice when he wrote on him in 1942, had been
superseded by one of open-eyed over-conscious apprehension.

IV Cecil Day Lewis

Self-division

Of the three Pylon poets who have written their auto-
biographies, Day Lewis tells us least. Stephen Spender's
World within a World is an essential part of his *oeuvre*,
while MacNeice's *The Strings Are False* proves a brilliant
tragic postscript. *The Buried Day* (1960) by Cecil Day
Lewis is more in the way of an adjunct, something to
supplement the verse — to explain it and "place" it in time.
This is not to say that its author practices the kind of
reserve and evasions that Robert Graves favors in *Good-
bye to All That*. *The Buried Day* does tell the poet's
story, both as to his public and private existence, and at
least up to his fifty-fifth birthday. What this book somehow
fails to do is to convey the feeling tone of the personality
we find in the verse, in the way in which Spender's or
MacNeice's life stories show themselves to be *extensions in
prose* of the person chiefly poetically expressive.

This is not to deny *The Buried Day* the status of an open
and an honest book (one suspects it could give points to
MacNeice on this score), but perhaps it tells us something
about the *kind* of poetry that Day Lewis writes whose
effects cannot be obtained in any medium save itself. That
poetry I would unhesitatingly call lyrical — a poetry of the
singing voice.

That the pitch of his verse has this instinctive quality,
this sense of spontaneity about it, does not in any way mean,
of course, that it springs from an undivided self or blithely
dismisses the dues of introspection. Indeed, the poet has
described himself as "a man who tends to be victimized
and activated, more than most perhaps, by inner conflict."
This inner conflict is very much the subject matter of his
first mature poems; but whereas with Spender a similar
self-division gives to his verse a reflective rhythm, tentative
and slow, the same inner questioning in Day Lewis fails to
retard the briskness of his verse. Perhaps this is another
way of saying that Day Lewis's poetry is more of a gift,
a windfall, a *donné* than with the other poets. ("For me,"

he tells us, "poetry comes and goes. I write verse quite prolifically for a year or two: then the impulse is exhausted . . . . These fallow times used to disquiet me, making me think I had run dry for ever, so that I questioned whether my way of life was the right one for a poet and would have changed it radically if I had known what way would be more productive.")

The poet was born at Batinbubber, Queen's County, Ireland on April 27, 1904. The natal dwelling, though "an unpretentious building . . . [had] elegance, and symmetry and a certain romantic charm." It looked, the poet afterwards concluded, "a large house to be occupied by a curate of the Church of Ireland whose income was about £150 a year."

An only child, who lost his mother when four years old, and was brought up largely in a world of adults, Day Lewis may be thought to have enjoyed, according to Cyril Connolly, that dubious privilege of genius: a deprived childhood.

At Sherborne and later at Wadham College, Oxford, Day Lewis has left a record of himself as the typical un-self-confident undergraduate, masking his social unsureness among richer, more worldly young men by participating in athletics. He was the only one of the Pylon poets to engage at the university in the so-called Philistine world of games.

A paradoxical figure

Cecil Day Lewis is a paradoxical figure. No one, among the Pylon poets, was so intransigent a foe to his own class, so much a hater of the bourgeoisie, so firmly committed to social revolution. Yet no other poet of this group in his war-time and postwar-time verse appeared to be writing so much out of the Romantic mandarin tradition — a tradition that included Virgil, Wordsworth, Clare, Hardy, Yeats, Valery, and Robert Frost. For most of these the Pylon poets in their early heyday had but scant respect.

This *volte-face* is not the reversal it may seem, at least not insofar as language is concerned. Looking back now at Day Lewis's early work, one sees how Auden's dictatorship of taste was seeking to impose on the slightly older poet a field of imagery partly alien to him. In poem after poem in Day Lewis's first phase one observes him gallantly

seeking to cope with images of an industrial order, only to
yield, before the end, to his own natural inclinations
toward imagery of a rural order.

"Let us be off" (from *The Magnetic Mountain*, 1933)
illustrates the poet's attempt to fight against his instinctive
choice in the selection of imagery. The poem, written in
couplets, falls into two sections. In the first, the terms of
reference are drawn from the field of railway engineering:

> Let us be off! Our steam
> Is deafening the dome.
> The needle in the gauge
> Points to a long-banked rage,
> And trembles there to show
> What a pressure's below.

But the second portion of the poem employs throughout a
pastoral frame of reference. Comparing the diction of the
two sections, one discovers a dichotomy more or less rigid;
for while the key words of the first are "Dome" (of a
locomotive), "gauge," "valve," "furnace," "coupling-rod,"
and "wheel," those of the second are "countryside," "daf-
fodils," "byre," "barrow," and "meadows" with a full
supporting cast of "poetic" adjectives: "honeyed," "golden,"
"wind-wanton," and "lovely."

The process one observes in this early poem is one we
see continued throughout the poet's career, with the second
field of imagery — the pastoral-agrarian — slowly taking
over the main work of expression as the influence of Virgil,
Frost, and Hardy gains and almost ousts that of Auden.

The poem, too, has a second surprise for us, since we
take it at first, in its context of the revolutionary thirties,
as a kind of allegorical journey from the capitalist in-
dustrialist present to a Utopian idyllic beauty. It is only
after we have read it carefully, noticing particularly its
concluding couplet

> Traveller, take care,
> Pick no flowers there!

that we realize it is a poem about love — about the act of
love in fact — and that the final reference is to the lover's
possessiveness concerning his beloved.

As Day Lewis has himself pointed out, "during my so-
called political period, most of my poems were in fact
about 'love or death'." This, perhaps, oversimplifies the
issue; but in retrospect it appears substantially correct.

From Feathers to Iron (1931) relates the story of how the poet and his wife wait over the months for their child to be born, just as *Transitional Poem* (1929) is the story of the attainment and triumph of love between a man and a woman. Both of these volumes do, indeed, carry a second or analogical meaning. The figure of the financier in the first poem is mocked by the poet who considers himself "capitalist/ In more intrinsic metal" (the private wealth of love, as distinct from the tycoon's power and possession often used to an antisocial end).

But *Transitional Poem* contains only hints of this, whereas *From Feathers to Iron* features the birth of a child as a revolutionary event: the miraculous victory of Eros and the life-force over Thanatos or death. Then, too, the language of this book shows us that Day Lewis was thinking of the child's birth as a microcosmic rebirth of society. In a poem that commemorates the child's safe delivery, the forces of industry are seen as receiving an influx of hope from this event:

> The nine tramp steamers rusting in the estuary
> Get up full pressure for a trade revival.

All the forces of nature, in fact, are requickened:

> Wherever radiance from ashes arises —
> Willowherb glowing on abandoned slagheaps,
> Dawn budding scarlet in a bed of darkness,
> Life from exhausted womb outstriving —
> There shall the spirit be lightened and gratefully
> Take a whole holiday in honour of this.

This "double image" of birth, as applied to the private and the public world, was something that Auden, the leader of the Pylon poets, had used in an extravagant, almost doggerel *Ode* celebrating the birth of a son to Rex Warner — a minor poet of the group, later to become an original novelist:

> Who'll save, who —
> Who'll save John Bull?
> From losing his wool.
> Now, Bull, now,
> I'll tell you who,
> I'll tell you how
> The flying stationer flies round the corner.
> Here it is, look! John, son of Warner,
> John, son of Warner, shall rescue you.
>   (from *The Orators*, 1932)

40

Day Lewis's poem pre-dates this, however.

The notion of birth as miraculous — as more than life-bringing in the obvious sense of the term — is the only parallel in Day Lewis that one discovers to the Christian story; unless one considers the "visiting angel, the strange new healer" (from "You that love England") — clearly a borrowing from Auden's Homer Lane-like psychiatrist figure, "each healer that in a city lives" — as a significant secular parallel to the Redeemer. It is, in any case, an image seldom occurring in Day Lewis.

Although Day Lewis's early poetry contains much angled partisan verse, and he had, as Robin Skelton remarks, "shown a tendency to place his trust in Marx first and the Muse second," by 1935 he was stating in his essay *Revolution in Poetry* that "A good poem . . . enters deep into the stronghold of our emotions: if it is written by a good revolutionary, it is bound to have a revolutionary effect on our emotions and therefore to be essentially — though not formally — propaganda." Robin Skelton's assessment of this statement appears to me a little naive. "This conclusion," he writes, "looks very much like a compromise arranged in order to give the poet the comfort of belonging to a 'movement' and the freedom to ignore its dogmas; it is one with the numerous attempts to prove that communism was the true heir to the liberal tradition."

To understand Day Lewis's predicament here, one must return to *Transitional Poem*, his first book in the "new" manner. Harking back to the English nature poets, he writes there how

> I could leave wonder on the latch
> And with a whole heart watch
> The calm declension of an English year.

Georgian in subject matter, though with an elegant metaphysical manner, he declares that

> I would be pedagogue — hear poplar, lime
> And oak recite the season's paradigm.

Yet this could only be his pleasant task:

> If I bricked up ambition and gave air
> To the ancestral curse that gabbles here

— the second line being, one assumes, a reference to the ill state of the economy and public health inherited from nineteenth century industrial England.

"Singing I was at peace," he tells us, yet with "A heart long sick for some Hesperides." But the very precariousness of this pre-partisan function (Morris's "idle singer of an empty day") of the poet — his isolation from the social issues of his time — lead him to confess in his poem *The Conflict*, written in 1933,

> I sang as one
> Who on a tilting deck sings
> To keep men's courage up, though the wave hangs
> That shall cut off their sun.

The poet envisages himself as fallen between the two stools of "neutrality" (the attitude of the French and British democracies) and "occupation" (the state of those Central European states already overrun by the totalitarian powers). For the independent artist, the uncommitted writer, Day Lewis believes there is no place:

> And private stars fade in the blood-red dawn
> Where two worlds strive.

The image of the red dawn (standing for the holocaust of war) leads the poet to other associations of the word "red": the solidarity of a Popular Front in which the forces of Communism stand for a new social future and opposition to the death cult of fascism:

> The red advance of life
> Contracts pride, calls out the common blood,
> Beats song into a single blade,
> Makes a depth-charge of grief.

The position reached in this poem represented the limit of Day Lewis's adherence to Socialist Realism. It led him to write (in *The Magnetic Mountain*) a number of knock-about propagandist pieces:

> Fireman and farmer, father and flapper,
> I'm speaking to you, sir, please drop that paper;
> Don't you know it's poison? Have you lost all hope?
> Aren't you ashamed, ma'am, to be taking dope?

These excoriations of the bourgeoisie in the admonitory manner of Auden were clearly a deflection of the poet's true muse, dissatisfaction with which led to the revised position set out in his essay *Revolution in Poetry*.

It is indicative of Day Lewis's real poetic gifts that the most successful pieces of social commentary he wrote took the form of traditional verse — even though his means of expression were those of parody. "A Carol" (with its wry presentation of an unemployed's Christmas), "Come live with me" (or love on the Means Test), and "I've heard them lilting" (courtship in the depressed areas) all take proverbially famous lyrics as a starting point for their criticism of society.

The transition, then, from Day Lewis's verse of social commentary (on socialist assumptions) to the verse of largely private experience which he wrote in his middle and later years, affords more continuity than might have been expected. The common element was traditional form, often partly disguised in the first phase, though as the poet observed, "contrary to received opinion about modern verse, nearly all my poems 'rhyme and scan'." Day Lewis has also remarked "how an over-enthusiastic, often perfunctory use of 'modern' imagery is gradually replaced by a more personal yet wider field of images."

In his volume *Wind over All* (1943), one sees Day Lewis's lyric gift (meaning, here, his gift for the short lyric poem) assuming its natural traditional form, both as to diction and imagery. Whereas in the verse of the thirties he had felt called upon to insert some contemporary reminder in the poem, he now felt at liberty to include or exclude it all. The poem "Hornpipe" makes mention of "esplanade," "speed-boats," and "wooden spades," but we are left with no precise twentieth century picture; only, in fact, with a nineteenth century music:

> Now the peak of summers' past, the sky is overcast
> And the love we swore would last for an age seems deceit:
> Paler is the gelder since the day we first beheld her
> In blush beside the elder drifting sweet, drifting sweet.

The heady rhythm, the floral imagery, the internal rhyme, and the last phrase repeated — these are some of the devices of Victorian lyric poetry, particularly of the Irish Victorians.

Day Lewis's lyric gift is a quality innate, yet one that also has been nourished by a number of other poets. His art of verbal assimilation is seen effectively in the fifth section of *An Italian Visit* (1953), in which famous Florentine pictures or sculpture are described in the manner of five *other* poets (Hardy, Yeats, Frost, Auden, Dylan Thomas). No piece, however, reveals this lyric quality better than the poem "Is it far to go?" The theme and convention of the compostion (a riddle about the nature of death) are traditional; and though Day Lewis's poem leans heavily on similar achievements in the past, it is marked by that sense of anonymity which is one of the marks of a certain type of lyric.

> Is it far to go?
>   A step — no further.
> Is it hard to go?
>   Ask the melting snow,
>   The eddying feather

might have been written at any time between the seventeenth century and today. In all the five stanzas of the poem, there is only one line ("Quick, Rose, and kiss me") that limits it to a Victorian or twentieth century statement. A poem of this kind is good solely because it seems to lack a signature.

During the war, he took to making translations from Virgil's poetry, finding his "imagination quickened and enriched by them." His version of the *Georgics* came in 1940, the *Aeneid* in 1952, and the *Eclogues* in 1963. In 1946, he also published his translation of Valery's *Le Cimitière Marin,* making by this gesture of attention and homage to the Symbolist past-master of Ivory Tower speech his final break with "the rather strident tub-thumping and pylon-praising" of his earlier verse. The ex-Communist new-Georgian had become a candidate for the Laureateship, to which he was appointed in 1968.

POSTSCRIPT

There is a question posited in the Harrow School Song relevant to these brief retrospections on the Pylon Poets of the 'Thirties: "How will it seem to us forty years on?"

Well, it is now — to be precise — thirty-nine years since Spender's hand-printed edition of Auden's first volume *Poems* appeared in 1930; and the whole tenor of our history and culture has changed.

Looking back on these poets — associated in their young pre-War prime with the literature of social revolution and change — the notion dawns that, today, their works are more rewardingly read in religious than in political terms. The fact that all three have remained "unbelievers" when set in the context of religious orthodoxy, with only the master-figure of Auden going on to become an Episcopalian, is perhaps what we should expect in a climate of opinion in which one speaks of a "layman's church" and "God without theology." Christians in Britain remember Dean Alec Vidler of Kings College, Cambridge, speaking in the 'Fifties of how he anticipated all the more interesting religious thought would, for a period, come *from outside the Church*.

To return, then, to the fanciful analogy employed at the beginning of this essay, we can see these poets, with the youthful Auden playing the role of a literary St. Paul, in the process of building a "secular church" — *a church of charity and unbelief.* Christ's command to "Love thy neighbor as thyself" was echoed by these poets in their attempt to remove those social and individual obstacles and inhibitions which impede, in Spender's words, "the palpable and obvious love of man for man." Spender, especially, has continued to assert the centrality of *caritas* or loving-kindness in any assessment of positive behavior or right disposition of heart. In a group of later poems, published between 1950 and 1953, he takes the image of his baby daughter crying in the night as a symbol of man's deprivation — of peace, love, harmony, rest, or ease:

> Listening, the parents know this primal cry
> Out of the gates of life, hollows such emptiness,
> It proves that all men's aims should be, all times,
> To fill the gap of pain with consolation.

In the same poem (*Nocturne*), Spender gets nearest to a concept of Original Sin. He envisages his child, who in addition to the dangers of nature, is vulnerable to "Man-made man-destroying ills." She is "subject to the rage of causes/ Dividing people" and leading to wars. Human love, in so far as it is possessive and exclusive, leads readily to destruction out of the desire to protect what is loved. And so Spender continues his argument:

> Even in this love
> Running in shoals on each side of her bed,
> Is fear and hate. If they [the parents] shift their glances
> From her who weeps, their eyes meet other eyes
> Willed with death, also theirs.

The answer to this predicament is the recognition of a distinction between *eros* and *agape*; or — to employ Auden's distinction — not the craving "to be loved alone" but "universal love." This may be taken as a commentary upon the limited slogan: "Make Love not War," but does show that the Flower-Children with their sometimes vague cult of loving could find much in these Pylon Poets still viable today.

SELECTED BIBLIOGRAPHY

GENERAL

Works

Oxford Poetry, with Introduction by W. H. Auden, Oxford, Blackwell 1927.

Poems by W. H. Auden, London, Faber 1930.

The Dog Beneath the Skin by W. H. Auden and Christopher Isherwood, London, Faber 1935 (verse drama).

The Ascent of F6 by W. H. Auden and Christopher Isherwood, London, Faber 1936 (verse drama).

On the Frontier by W. H. Auden and Christopher Isherwood, London, Faber 1938 (verse drama).

Journey to a War by W. H. Auden and Christopher Isherwood, London, Faber 1939 (a prose and verse travelogue).

Letters from Iceland by W. H. Auden and L. MacNeice, London, Faber 1936 (a prose and verse travelogue).

New Year Letter by W. H. Auden, London, Faber 1941.

Criticism

Auden and After by Francis Scarfe, London, Routledge 1942.

The Modern Writer and His Work by G. S. Fraser, London, Penguin 1964.

Vision and Rhetoric by G. S. Fraser, London, Faber 1959.

A Vision of Reality by Frederick Grubb, London, Chatto & Windus 1965.

Auden by Richard Hogart, London, Chatto & Windus 1951.

STEPHEN SPENDER

Works

Collected Poems, London, Faber 1954.

Twenty Poems, privately printed 1930.

Poems, London, Faber 1933.

Vienna, London, Faber 1934 (verse drama).

Forward from Liberalism, London, Gollancz 1935 (prose).

Trial of a Judge, London, Faber 1938 (verse drama).

The Still Centre, London, Faber 1939.

Ruins and Visions, London, Faber 1942.

Poems of Dedication, London, Faber 1942.

The Edge of Being, London, Faber 1949.

World within a World, London, Hamilton 1951 (autobiography).

The Creative Element, London, Hamilton 1953 (criticism).

The Making of a Poem, London, Hamilton 1955 (criticism).

Criticism

The first three critical titles listed in the "General" section all have essays or passages on Spender.

Works

Collected Poems, London, Faber 1966.

The Agamemnon of Aeschylus, London, Faber 1936 (translation).

I Crossed the Minch, London, Faber 1938 (reportage).

Modern Poetry, London, Macmillan 1935 (criticism).

Autumn Journal, London, Faber 1939.

W. B. Yeats, London, Macmillan 1941 (criticism).

Plant and Phantom. London, Faber 1941.

The Dark Tower and Other Radio Scripts, London, Faber 1947 (drama).

The Burnt Offerings, London, Faber 1951.

Autumn Sequences, London, Faber 1954.

Visitations, London, Faber 1957.

Solstices, London, Faber 1961.

The Burning Perch, London, Faber 1963.

The Strings Are False, London, Faber 1965 (autobiography).

Varieties of Parable, London, Cambridge University Press 1965 (criticism).

Criticism

The first three critical titles listed in the "General" section all have essays or passages on MacNeice.

Louis MacNeice by John Press, London, Longmans Green 1967.

CECIL DAY LEWIS

Works

Collected Poems, London, Cape & Hogarth Press 1954.

A Hope for Poetry, Oxford, Basil Blackwell 1934 (criticism).

Overtures to Death, London, Cape 1938.

Word Overall, London, Cape 1943.

The Poetic Image, London, Cape 1947 (criticism).

The Poet's Task, Oxford, Oxford University Press 1951 (criticism).

An Italian Visit, London, Cape 1953.

The Buried Day, London, Chatto & Windus 1960 (autobiography).

The Aenead of Virgil, London, Hogarth Press 1952 (translation).

The Eclogues of Virgil, London, Cape 1963 (translation).

Criticism

C. Day Lewis by Clifford Dyment, London, Longmans Green 1955.

Auden and After by Francis Scarfe, London, Routledge 1942.

The Modern Writer and His World by G. S. Fraser, London, Penguin 1964. (This contains a passage on C. Day Lewis.)

P 416
8

60 48 9

DATE DUE

JOSTEN'S 30 508